Forest and Vale and High Blue Hill

To Gillian, and to Alan, my father and
in memory of my mother Peggy

FOREST AND VALE AND HIGH BLUE HILL

Poems of Gloucestershire, the Cotswolds and Beyond

Selected by Johnny Coppin

◆

Wood Engravings by Ray Hedger

THE WINDRUSH PRESS · GLOUCESTERSHIRE

First published in 1991 by
The Windrush Press
Windrush House
Main Street
Adlestrop
Moreton-in-Marsh
Gloucestershire GL56 0YN

Telephone: 0608 658075
Fax: 0608 658860

Introduction and Selection © Johnny Coppin 1991
Illustrations © Ray Hedger 1991

British Library Cataloguing in Publication Data
A catalogue record for this book is
available from the British Library

ISBN 0 900075 17 1

Printed and bound in Great Britain by Biddles Ltd, Guildford

CONTENTS

SUMMER

AUTUMN

WINTER

FOREWORD

This anthology, enhanced with wood-engravings by Ray Hedger, is not just another romantic miscellany of country poems, but a rich harvest culled from some ten years of reading and collecting Gloucestershire poets and poetry. I know that much dedicated work has marked and informed this quest – reading, re-reading, weeding, doubting and deciding – for over the past ten years or so, Johnny Coppin has haunted the bookshops in the Cotswolds looking for small volumes of verse that would fit his theme, both major and minor poets. I remember many of his visits to my bookshop, and in particular the day he came in to find a large collection of books by Leonard Clark, mostly inscribed presentation copies, some of which he could afford at the time, while other ephemeral items I saved until funds were available again. I imagine that his collection must be very comprehensive and am delighted that, out of the hundreds of poems he might have been tempted to include, he has been fairly ruthless and only allowed the best through his seasonal mesh.

Looking back through my files of the Cheltenham Festival of Literature, I see that it was in 1983 that the Festival premiered Johnny Coppin's 'Forest and Vale and High Blue Hill', his seasonal song cycle of poems by many of the area's best poets. This anthology springs directly from that evocative composition.

As I read these poems I feel an affinity with Johnny, for when, in 1984, I was planning the 1985 Festival of Literature, I had some rather grandiose thoughts of basing the whole festival on the 'Literary View from the Hills'. So I spent many early morning hours walking on Leckhampton and Cleeve Hill, dreaming up ideas, talking to myself or my dog about this spacious and evocative theme, one in which the tutelary deity of place would be looked at and celebrated. I made a list of some 120 authors who would easily fit into this framework; from Kilvert to Housman, F.W. Harvey to Dennis Potter, Massingham to John Moore, P.J. Kavanagh to L.T.C Rolt, Laurie Lee to Ursula

Fanthorpe, and of course all the poets in this book. *Genius loci* became an obsession for a few months, but it became too vast a theme to fulfil, and finally became 'The Spirit of Place in Literature'.

So it has been, in a quieter and more methodical way with Johnny Coppin, or so I imagine. He too had an obsession, one which has finally come to fruition in this book, an anthology which I hope and believe will have the 'timeless quality of a flowering hedgerow' as well as 'the smooth-wrapped hardness of moss-dressed stone' as the senior living poet in this book so elegantly puts it.

Alan Hancox
Cheltenham 1991

INTRODUCTION

I so clearly remember my first vivid impressions of the Cotswolds and Gloucestershire, as I travelled by train from Paddington to Cheltenham many years ago. As the train sped along the single track from Swindon, across the hills and down into the Stroud Valley, time appeared to stand still, and the villages and farms seemed to grow out of the landscape. The wonder of those first images is with me still, and has been matched only by the excitement of discovering so many beautiful poems about the area many years later.

This anthology is a very personal selection and reflects my own preference for poetry from the twentieth century (with the exception of some poems by William Morris that were inspired by Kelmscott Manor, near Lechlade – his 'grey old house by the water'). Although Cotswold and Gloucestershire poems have been written for centuries, I have mostly chosen those written in the language of today – poems that speak to me most directly.

Over the years I have been particularly drawn to the work of Laurie Lee, Ivor Gurney, F.W. Harvey, and Leonard Clark. I have enjoyed setting many of their poems to music, and it is natural, therefore, that their work forms the heart of this collection. In Laurie Lee's poetry we have powerful images and passion rooted in the Slad Valley, deep in the Cotswolds; Gurney and Harvey, who were close friends and both from the Vale of Gloucester, were 'homesick for their hills' during and after the First World War, and show a remarkable range and depth in their poetry; and Leonard Clark displays a beautiful lyrical style with his finely detailed observations of life in the Forest of Dean.

Over the years I have collected so many wonderful poems from the area that, in making this selection, it has been very hard to decide what to leave out. I very much wanted to present the anthology as a seasonal cycle, and I hope that, within this self-imposed but natural structure, I have shown the full range of poetry from the area: from the turn-of-the-century poems of Masefield, Davies, Drinkwater and other

1

'Dymock Poets', right through to the modern work of Charles Tomlinson, P.J. Kavanagh, U.A. Fanthorpe, Frances and Michael Horovitz, and many others.

I feel I must give some background information in tracing the origins of this collection. It was back in 1965 that I caught the train from my native London to study architecture at the College of Art in Cheltenham, and it is there that I started my musical career with the band Decameron in the early seventies. Gradually I began to appreciate Gloucestershire and the Cotswolds more fully; to know its secret valleys, tiny churches, and the contrasts of its seasons, and also to understand its deep sense of history and how this has shaped the England of today. I soon began to realise how the landscape has been, and still is, such an inspiration to generations of musicians, artists, designers, craftsmen, and particularly poets and writers.

Shortly after starting my solo career in the late seventies, I was lucky enough to hear Laurie Lee and Frank Mansell at a poetry reading. This led me to recording my setting of Frank Mansell's 'The Roads Go Down' on my first album *Roll on Dreamer*, and the song has proved to be very popular. Then, in 1982, I began to search for more local poems to set to music, and was amazed to discover the little-known work of Gurney, Harvey, Clark, and many others. The more poems I discovered, the more I identified with them and with their celebration of Gloucestershire and the Cotswolds. I became convinced that everyone with a love of the region should be aware of and enjoy these poems, and so, beginning with Leonard Clark's 'This Night The Stars', I started to turn many of them into songs.

The result was the album *Forest and Vale and High Blue Hill* which was launched at the Cheltenham Festival of Literature in 1983. The title is a line from Harvey's poem 'A Song of Gloucestershire', and so aptly describes the three distinct areas of the region – the Forest of Dean, the Vale of Severn, and the Cotswold Hills. The songs are timeless, and seem to strike a chord with people everywhere, and not just in the West Country. This was to lead to my own national BBC TV programme *A Song of Gloucestershire* (directed by Mike Dornan) in 1986, and based entirely on songs and poets featured on the album.

Further research and the setting of more poems was to result in my recording the *English Morning* album in 1987, and then in 1989 I was especially pleased to be able to collaborate with Laurie Lee on the album *Edge of Day*, a seasonal cycle in words and music, and a tribute to his wonderful poetry. Since then I have enjoyed recording more Gloucestershire and Cotswold poems for *The Glorious Glosters* album (with the Band of the Glos. Regiment), and for the musical drama *Songs on Lonely Roads*, the story of composer and poet Ivor Gurney (with actor, writer, and good friend David Goodland).

So now at last, after years of collecting poems from the area, my dream of an anthology has come true. I am indebted to so many people – first and foremost to my wife Gillian for her love and understanding, and for sharing the dream; and then to Victoria Huxley and Geoffrey Smith of Windrush Press for realising the project.

The book is designed to be either read in seasonal order or to be dipped into. Some of the poems are newly discovered, but many of them I have loved and lived with for many years. I do hope they will give you as much pleasure as they have given me.

Johnny Coppin
Gloucestershire, June 1991

ACKNOWLEDGEMENTS

In guiding and helping me in my research I sincerely thank Alan Hancox, Alan Tucker, and Douglas McLean (and their bookshops in Cheltenham, Stroud, and Coleford); Rosealeen Lane, Neville Chapman, and the staff at Gloucester Library; Michael Darling and the staff at Cheltenham Library; and staff at the Bristol, Bath, and Oxford Libraries.

For their encouragement and support from the outset and along the way I thank all my (immediate) family – my father, my brothers Julian, and Richard and his family, John, Philomena, and Martin Wall, Pamela and Joshua Dempsey – and the following friends and fellow-musicians: Phil Beer and Anna Spacey, Paul and Jane Burgess, Mick Dolan and Glen Goodman, Matt Clifford, Bob and Nancy Clifford, Steve Hutt and Cherrylou Skiff, David Goodland and Brian Wheeler, Mike and Régine Candler, Kathy van den Elst, Jerry and Anna Friar, Chris Eldon-Lee and Sue Herbert, Jane and Martin Fry, Beth and Martin Whittaker, Al and Jenny Fenn, Geoff and Frankie March, David and Mathilda Bell, Dik and Barbara Cadbury, Anthony and Anne Boden, Trevor and Caroline Foster, John and Gill Broomhall, Gareth Sampson, Malcolm and Ann Kilminster, Maureen, Freiden and Colette Darwin, Jenny and David Williams, Margaret and Brian Scragg, Jon and Nicky Davison, John and Cathy Eeles, Dave and Carole Cartwright, Margaret Austin, Jon and Annie Acock, Lynn Holmes, Mimi Pfeifer, and Ruth, Peter, Jane, and Christopher Dawson.

Thank you to Ray Hedger for interpreting and capturing the spirit of the poems so well in his delightful wood-engravings.

For their continual support I thank Eddie Vickers and Severn Sound radio; Mike D'Abo, Geraldine McCullagh, Andy Vivien, Rob Salvidge, and Mark Hurrell and all at BBC Radio Gloucestershire; The Cheltenham Festival of Literature; Mike Dornan of BBC TV (and his wife Carol) for the *Song of Gloucestershire* programme; Simon Hammond of BBC TV; Ken Price, Bryan Izzard, Jeffrey Milland, Lesley

Morgan, and Richard Wyatt and all at HTV; Geoff Barratt and Ken Goodwin of Central TV; Frank and Joanna Hopkinson for the video of the song 'Warning'; John Turner, Keith Warmington, Roger Bennett, Vicki Klein and all at BBC Radio Bristol; Alan Roberts and Neil George of Radio 2; Andy Westgate of GWR radio; Chris Eldon-Lee, Richard Walker, and Mike Naylor of BBC Radio Shropshire; Nonny Dumville of BBC Hereford and Worcester; Jon Benns of BBC Radio South and West; Geoff Blake of Plymouth Sound; and Gary Price and Roger Watson of BBC Radio Oxford.

For their help and understanding in dealing with permissions, I thank Penny Ely (Trustee of the Gurney Estate), the late Robin Haines, Robert Clark, Patrick Harvey, Eileen Griffiths, Patrick Dobell, Mrs Brenda Deans, Mrs Freda Hastings, Douglas Bird, Felicité Nesham and the Severn Springs Adventure Playground, and Penny Drinkwater Self. I thank the following for their wonderful poems: Laurie Lee, Charles Tomlinson, Michael Horovitz, P.J. Kavanagh, U.A. Fanthorpe, Jim Turner, Les Arnold, Joyce Latham, Sheila Simmons, and David Ashbee.

Johnny Coppin
Gloucestershire, June 1991

CREDITS

The publishers would like to credit and thank the following for their kind permission in allowing the use of the poems in this anthology. While every effort has been made to contact the copyright holders the publishers would be happy to hear from anyone whom they have not been able to trace. Mr Jeffrey Cooper for the extract from 'Ryton Firs' by Lascelles Abercrombie, from *Twelve Idylls* published by Martin Secker, 1928. Les Arnold for 'The Brassrubbing' from *The Sheep Pen*, 1982. David Ashbee and *Gloucestershire and Avon Life* for 'Cotswolds' from *Perpetual Waterfalls*, Enitharmon Press, 1989. John Murray (Publishers) Ltd for extract from *Summoned by Bells* by John Betjeman, 1960. Peters, Fraser & Dunlop Group Ltd, for extract from 'Dedicatory Ode' from *The Complete Verse of Hilaire Belloc* published by Pimlico Books, a division of Random Century. Clarissa Mitchell on behalf of The Gloucester Special Adventure Playground Association for 'Cotswold Tiles' by Edward Berryman from *Nursery Rhymes of Gloucestershire*. The Literary Executor of Leonard Clark for the poems of Leonard Clark: 'This Night The Stars' from *The County Series of Contemporary Poetry VII: Gloucester*, 1927; 'The Wood', 'The Hill', and 'Have Wandered' from *English Morning and Other Poems*, Hutchinson, 1953; 'Singing in the Streets' from *Singing in the Streets*, Dobson Books, 1972; and extract from 'Cider-House' from *The Way It Was*, Enitharmon Press, 1980. Andrew Dalby for 'Roel Gate' and 'Springtime in December' by Arthur Dalby. W.H. Davies: 'Nailsworth Hill' and 'The Villain' from *Collected Poems*, Jonathan Cape, 1942. Patrick Dobell for 'Briar Roses' and 'Cotswold Roads' by Eva Dobell from *A Bunch of Cotswold Grasses*, 1919. John Drinkwater: 'Cotswold Love', 'Legacy', and 'The Cotswold Farmers' from *Tides*, Sidgwick & Jackson, 1917; and 'Sonnet' from *Summer Harvest*, Sidgwick & Jackson, 1933. Harry Chambers, The Peterloo Poets for 'On Buying OS Sheet 163' by U.A. Fanthorpe from *Standing To*, The Peterloo Poets, 1982. James Elroy Flecker: 'November Eves' from *Selected Poems*, Martin

Secker, 1918. Patrick Flower for 'The Forest of Dean' by Robin Flower. Penny Ely, Sole Trustee of the Gurney Estate for the use of Ivor Gurney poems from *Collected Poems of Ivor Gurney* ed. P.J. Kavanagh, Oxford University Press, 1982; and 'The Fisherman of Newnham' from *War's Embers*, Sidgwick & Jackson, 1919 and Carcanet Press, 1987. Pamela Haines for 'The High-Road' by John Haines from *Poems*, Selwyn & Blount, 1921. P.W. Harvey for the poems of F.W. Harvey: 'A Song of Gloucestershire', 'Piper's Wood', 'In Flanders' and 'Triolet' from *A Gloucestershire Lad at Home & Abroad*, Sidgwick & Jackson, 1916 and Douglas McLean, 1988; 'Gloucestershire From The Train' from *Farewell*, Sidgwick & Jackson, 1921; 'Spring 1924', 'Swift Beauty', and 'September' from *September and Other Poems*, Sidgwick & Jackson, 1925. Bloodaxe Books for permission to quote from *Collected Poems* by Frances Horovitz, published 1985. Michael Horovitz for extract from *Midsummer Morning Jog Log*, Five Seasons Press, Hereford, 1986; and 'A Ghost of Summer' from *Growing Up: Selected Poems & Pictures*, Alison & Busby, 1979. P.J. Kavanagh for 'News from Gloucestershire' from *Life Before Death*, Chatto & Windus, 1979. Joyce Latham for 'Autumn Swan Song' from *Puzzlewood and Other Poems* published by D. McLean, Forest Bookshop, 1979. Peters, Fraser & Dunlop Group Ltd. for poems by Laurie Lee from *Selected Poems*, published by André Deutsch, 1983. The Literary Executors of Frank Mansell for his poems from *Cotswold Ballads*, Richard Courtauld, 1974. The Society of Authors, the literary representative of the Estate of John Masefield for extract from 'The Everlasting Mercy' and 'Tewkesbury Road' from *Collected Poems*, Heinemann, 1923. William Morris: extract from 'June' from *The Earthly Paradise*, Kelmscott Press, 1868/70; and extract from *The Story of the Glittering Plain*, Kelmscott Press, 1891. Edward Shanks: 'Dover's Hill' from *Collected Poems 1909-1925*, Collins, 1926. Sheila Simmons for 'Spring Day, Cheltenham' and 'June Evening, Stroud Valley'. Edward Thomas: 'Adlestrop' from *Collected Poems*, Selwyn & Blount, 1928. Oxford University Press for poems © Charles Tomlinson 1985, reprinted from Charles Tomlinson's *Collected Poems*, 1985. Jim Turner for his poems from *Lost Days* published by the Whittington Press. Brian Waters: 'This Ancient Wall' from *The Golden Oriole and Other Poems*, Shakespeare Head Press/ Blackwell, 1938. David Higham Associates for extract from *The Island* by Francis Brett Young, published by Heinemann Ltd, 1944.

7

A Song of Gloucestershire

(dedicated to the Glos. Society)

North, South, East, and West:
Think of whichever you love the best.
Forest and vale and high blue hill:
You may have whichever you will,
And quaff one cup to the love o' your soul
Before we drink to the lovely whole.

Here are high hills with towns all stone,
(Did you come from the Cotswolds then?)
And an architecture all their own,
  And a breed of sturdy men.

But here's a forest old and stern,
(Say, do you know the Wye?)
Where sunlight dapples green miles of fern,
  A river wandering by.

Here's peaceful meadow-land and kine,
(Do you see a fair grey tower?)
Where sweet together close entwine
  Grass, clover, and daisy flower.

Here stretches the land towards the sea,
(Behold the castle bold!)
Where men live out life merrily,
  And die merry and old.

North, South, East, and West:
Think of whichever you love the best.
Forest and vale and high blue hill:
You may have whichever you will,
And quaff one cup to the love o' your soul
  Before we drink to the lovely whole.

F.W. HARVEY

SPRING

In March

These dry, bright winter days,
　　When the crow's colour takes to itself
Such gloss, the shadows from the hedge
　　Ink-stain half way across
The road to where a jagged blade
　　Of light eats into them: light's guarded frontier
Is glittering everywhere, everywhere held
　　Back by naked branchwork, dark
Fissurings along the creviced walls,
　　Shade side of barn and house, of half-cut stack
Strawing the ground, in its own despite
　　With flecks of pallid gold, allies to light:
And over it all, a chord of glowing black
　　A shining, flying shadow, the crow is climbing.

CHARLES TOMLINSON

Spring 1924

Spring came by water to Broadoak this year.
I saw her clear.
Though on the earth a sprinkling
Of snowdrops shone, the unwrinkling
Bright curve of Severn River
Was of her gospel first giver.
Like a colt new put to pasture it galloped on;
And a million
Small things on its back for token
Of her coming it bore. A broken
Hawthorn floated green,
Gem-bright upon the sheen
Of the moving water. There past
Hay-wisps which showed the fast
Of winter was over for cattle,
Who needed no longer battle
For food in some far meadow.
Soft as shadow
There glided past a skiff,
Heavy with mended nets for salmon. If
Spring dreamed
Lazily in Earth's half-frozen blood,
On Severn's flood
Her presence bravely gleamed.
Yea, all who sought her
Might see, wondering, how Spring walked the water.

F.W. HARVEY

There Was Such Beauty

There was such beauty in the dappled valley
As hurt the sight, as stabbed the heart to tears.
The gathered loveliness of all the years
Hovered thereover, it seemed, eternally
Set for men's joy. Town, tower, trees, river
Under a royal azure sky for ever
Up-piled with snowy towering bulks of cloud:
A herald-day of spring more wonderful
Than her true own. Trumpets cried aloud
In sky, earth, blood; no beast, no clod so dull
But the power felt of the day, and of the giver
Was glad for life, humble at once and proud.
Kyrie Eleison, and Gloria,
Credo, Jubilate, Magnificat:
The whole world gathered strength to praise the day.

IVOR GURNEY

Piper's Wood

In Minsterworth when March is in,
   And Spring begins to gild the days,
Oh! then starts up a joyous din,
   For Piper's Wood is full of praise,
Because the birds deem winter gone
And welcome the returning sun.

Blackbird and thrush and robin dear
   Within that wood try over all
The songs they mean to shout so clear
   Before green leaves grow red and fall;
And harkening in its shadows you
Must needs sing out of Summer too.

F.W. HARVEY

Spring Day, Cheltenham

The sunlight has an edge to it today,
the busy Spa is sparkling.
A springtime fever has set in
and flocks of shoppers
flaunt fine feathers
in the hopeful air.
Shop windows issue challenges, swiftly caught up;
the ordered traffic glints and hums,
those pale palladian palaces
(now office blocks and flats!)
gleam cleanly, and compose
a gracious and sophisticated urban scene.

But in the middle of it all
high in the peeling plane-trees on the Promenade
a ragamuffin enclave
carries on its raucous rural life
regardless!
          Rooks. . . .

                    rearing their young
                      on tottering airy rafts;
heedlessly dropping feathers, sticks
(and worse than sticks!)
on the prim pavements;
filling the seemly air with strident exclamation;
flying and foraging
as if the smart and fashionable town
were still a village street
with new-ploughed fields and Cotswold sheep
only a step away.

SHEILA SIMMONS

The Fisherman of Newnham

When I was a boy at Newnham,
  For every tide that ran
Swift on its way to Bollo,
  I wished I were a man
To sail out and discover
  Where such a tide began.

But when my strength came on me
  'Tis I must earn my bread:
My Father set me fishing
  By Frampton Hock, instead
Of wandering to the ocean –
  Wherever Severn led.

And now I've come to manhood,
  Too many cares have I
To think of gallivanting
  (A wife and child forbye).
So I must wonder ever
  Until time comes to die.

Then I shall question Peter
  Upon the heavenly floor,
What makes the tide in rivers –
  How comes the Severn bore,
And all things he will tell me
  I never knew before.

IVOR GURNEY

from *Ryton Firs*

From Marcle way,
From Dymock, Kempley, Newent, Bromesberrow,
Redmarley, all the meadowland daffodils seem
Running in golden tides to Ryton Firs,
To make the knot of steep little wooded hills
Their brightest show: *O bella età de l'oro!*
Now I breathe you again, my woods of Ryton:
Not only golden with your daffodil light
Lying in pools on the loose dusky ground
Beneath the larches, tumbling in broad rivers
Down sloping grass under the cherry trees
And birches: but among your branches clinging
A mist of that Ferrara-gold I first
Loved in those easy hours you made so green.

LASCELLES ABERCROMBIE

The Order of Saying

'As soon as the blackthorn comes in flower
    The wind blows cold,' she says:
I see those bushes tossed and whitening,
    Drawing the light and currents of the air
Into their mass and depth; can only see
    The order of her saying in that flare
That rises like a beacon for the wind
    To flow into, to twist and wear
Garment and incandescence, flag of spring.

CHARLES TOMLINSON

April Rise

If ever I saw blessing in the air
   I see it now in this still early day
Where lemon-green the vaporous morning drips
   Wet sunlight on the powder of my eye.

Blown bubble-film of blue, the sky wraps round
   Weeds of warm light whose every root and rod
Splutters with soapy green, and all the world
   Sweats with the bead of summer in its bud.

If ever I heard blessing it is there
   Where birds in trees that shoals and shadows are
Splash with their hidden wings and drops of sound
   Break on my ears their crests of throbbing air.

Pure in the haze the emerald sun dilates,
   The lips of sparrows milk the mossy stones,
While white as water by the lake a girl
   Swims her green hand among the gathered swans.

Now, as the almond burns its smoking wick,
   Dropping small flames to light the candled grass;
Now, as my low blood scales its second chance,
   If ever world were blessèd, now it is.

LAURIE LEE

The Roman Villa – Chedworth

Did Tribune or Centurion
   Find solace in a British home
Where colder Cotswold rivers run,
   Far from the Tiber, far from Rome?

Would tired, aching eyelids close –
   Weary of Legions' endless march –
And sandalled feet find lost repose
   Under the slender hazels' arch?

In mossy earth the seekers find
   Buckle and brooch that decked a bride
Whose alien thought perplexed his mind,
   Whose Celtic beauty snared his pride.

The bluebell tide still drowns the wood.
   Hidden, the valley-lily lies
Where arum folds its secret hood.
   Pale primroses spread paradise.

The withered bracken's russet lace
   Curtains the grave where ages rust.
The flowers that jewel this English place
   Soon mingle with the Roman dust.

JIM TURNER

20

The Wood

There was a wood of beech trees near my home
Whose roots were twisted round the pitted rocks,
And in the branches every spring
The thrushes sang so constantly
The glens became a single chord of sound.
The sun lay all along the faces of the leaves
And on the swinging rows of scentless flowers;
The wood stretched far into the silences,
But as you leaped from rock to rock, you heard
The tiny notes of water dripping on bright stones
And orchestras of insects underground,
You saw the ferns uncurling baby fronds
And sudden islands of forget-me-nots.
And when at last you reached the circling wire
That cut in two this trembling forest world,
You plunged into a hundred seas of bluebell light
And like a crazy traveller drugged and lost
In undiscovered continents,
You sank, defeated, drenched with flowers,
Beneath the drowning tides that wandered there.

LEONARD CLARK

21

Sonnet
(To Tanya – Fairford, April 1926)

We have laid up simples against forgetfulness,
For we the nesting missel-thrush have seen
Brooding above the weaving watercress;
We have gone by water-meadows fresh and green
Studded with kingcups and with cuckoo-flowers,
By hedges newly fledged with blackthorn foam,
And rested, weary with the happy hours,
At twilight by the kindled hearth of home.

This was our spring, our lucky Eastertide,
By willowed brooks, and from a western shire
We shared a Monday of the undaunted pride
Of him who sang the old, the heart's desire;
England we were; and yet of England own
The budding bough, the song, the builded stone.

JOHN DRINKWATER

The Tree

Day-long the shapely flowering tree
   Sparkled beneath the April sun,
Its garlands stirring ceaselessly,
     Wind-pestered till the day was done:
       A lovely tree, radiant and rare,
       Full-flowered in beauty, fair, so fair.

Now that the daylight falls to night,
   And stills the wind that plagued the day,
The flowered tree – a week's delight –
     Shadows its silver store away.
       As dusk slips tranquil from the hill,
       The fair tree stands so still, so still.

Night hesitates behind the day,
   Blossoms still glimmer on the grass;
The faltering twilight steps away
     To let her sombre sister pass.
       At last, night-wrapped, the tree will keep
       Its loveliness, asleep . . . asleep.

JIM TURNER

Cotswold Love

Blue skies are over Cotswold
   And April snows go by,
The lasses turn their ribbons
   For April's in the sky,
And April is the season
   When Sabbath girls are dressed,
From Rodboro' to Campden,
   In all their silken best.

An ankle is a marvel
   When first the buds are brown,
And not a lass but knows it
   From Stow to Gloucester town.
And not a girl goes walking
   Along the Cotswold lanes
But knows men's eyes in April
   Are quicker than their brains.

It's little that it matters,
   So long as you're alive,
If you're eighteen in April,
   Or rising sixty-five,
When April comes to Amberley
   With skies of April blue,
And Cotswold girls are briding
   With slyly tilted shoe.

JOHN DRINKWATER

The Hill

I remember a hill where plum trees flowered
Heavy and white at the ending of spring,
And after them the pear trees followed
So that the hill was never without its snow.
The orchards there were huddled round cottages
Beneath whose twittering thatch green wood fires burned,
And all along the avenues squealed bulging sows
To scatter far the gossiping hens and cockerel.
Old men in clogs and fusty corduroy
Sharpened their scythes with sparking stones
Or padded about the sweet, dark cider mills;
With sudded arms blue-aproned women came
To hang out new-washed clothes
Upon the branches of far whiter trees.
And on the turf that climbed the brackened hill
The coarse-woolled sheep tugged solemnly all day
And were as free as air.
But most of all I think of one dead, cloven tree
Between whose mated forks
You saw a hundred clover fields away
The great strong bow of Severn winding out to sea
And Gloucester tower foursquare and shining in the Cotswold sky.

LEONARD CLARK

The Incense Bearers

Toward the sun the drenched May-hedges lift
White rounded masses like still ocean-drift,
And day fills with heavy scent of that gift.

There is no escaping that full current of thick
Incense; one walks, suddenly one comes quick
Into a flood of odour there, aromatic,

Not English; for cleaner, sweeter, is the hot scent that
Is given from hedges, solitary flowers, not
In mass, but lonely odours that scarcely float.

But the incense bearers, soakers of sun's full
Powerfulness, give out floods unchecked, wonderful
Utterance almost, which makes no poet grateful,

Since his love is for single things rarely found,
Or hardly: violets blooming in remote ground,
One colour, one fragrance, like one uncompanied sound

Struck upon silence, nothing looked-for. Hung
As from gold wires this May incense is swung,
Heavy of odour, the drenched meadows among.

IVOR GURNEY

from *Summoned by Bells*

Oxford May mornings! When the prunus bloomed
We'd drive to Sunday lunch at Sezincote:
First steps in learning how to be a guest,
First wood-smoke-scented luxury of life
In the large ambience of a country house.
Heavy with hawthorn scent were Cotswold lanes,
Golden the church towers standing in the sun,
And Gordon Russell with his arts and crafts,
Somewhere beyond in Broadway. Down the drive,
Under the early yellow leaves of oaks;
One lodge is Tudor, one in Indian Style.

The bridge, the waterfall, the Temple Pool –
And there they burst on us, the onion domes,
Chajjahs and chattris made of amber stone:
'Home of the Oaks', exotic Sezincote!
Stately and strange it stood, the Nabob's house,
Indian without and coolest Greek within,
Looking out from Gloucestershire to Oxfordshire;
And, by supremest landscape-gardener's art,
The lake below the eastward slope of grass
Was made to seem a mighty river-reach
Curving along to Chipping Norton's hills.

*

At six o'clock from Bourton-on-the-Hill
The bells rang out above the clumps of oak;
A lighter peal from Longborough lingered on;
Moreton-in-Marsh came echoing from the vale . . .
So gently broke the triple waves of sound
On a still evening of enormous light
That, when they ceased, I almost seemed to hear
From open church-doors village voluntaries
A mile and more away.

JOHN BETJEMAN

The Forest of Dean

The quiet congregation of the trees
Awoke to a rippled whisper. The light winged breeze
Brushed leaf against leaf, softly and delicately fingering
Silken beech and ragged oak leaf; and in the cool shadow
And wavering dapple of tremulous sunlight lingering
As weary of the hot gold glow of the buttercup meadow,
And renewing his strength in the cool green and still shade
Of the forest, deeper and deeper burrowing in
By pathway and trackway and green ride and arched glade
Over hyacinth and the white starred garlic and curled fern,
And dreaming in some unvisited haven to win
New life from the growing grass and rejoicing return
To sweep from hill to valley, from valley to hill.
The birds were still,
Only far-off a cuckoo calling,
Drowsily and perpetually a far-off cuckoo calling.

ROBIN FLOWER

The Roads Go Down

The roads go down to Gloucester town
 And Severn seeks the sea;
But what road leads where I'd be gone,
 What river flows to thee?

In stalwart band the beeches stand
 Above the sheltered ground;
But in what haven, in what land,
 Shall vanished hope be found?

White bloomed the thorn on that May morn,
 Sweet called the velvet dove;
Like rippling breeze on young green corn
 Was the caress of love.

The daylight fails and in the vales
 The lamps of evening shine;
Where is the ship with many sails
 Shall link thy fate and mine?

The roads go down to Gloucester town
 And Severn seeks the sea;
But no road leads where I'd be gone,
 No river flows to thee.

FRANK MANSELL

SUMMER

The Edge of Day

The dawn's precise pronouncement waits
With breath of light indrawn,
Then forms with smoky, smut-red lips
The great O of the sun.

The mouldering atoms of the dark
Blaze into morning air;
The birdlike stars droop down and die,
The starlike birds catch fire.

The thrush's tinder throat strikes up,
The sparrow chips hot sparks
From flinty tongue, and all the sky
Showers with electric larks.

And my huge eye a chaos is
Where molten worlds are born;
Where floats the eagle's flaming moon,
And crows, like clinkers, burn;

Where blackbirds scream with comet tails,
And flaring finches fall,
And starlings, aimed like meteors,
Bounce from the garden wall;

Where, from the edge of day I spring
Alive for mortal flight,
Lit by the heart's exploding sun
Bursting from night to night.

LAURIE LEE

Tewkesbury Road

It is good to be out on the road, and going one knows
    not where,
  Going through meadow and village, one knows not
    whither nor why;
Through the grey light drift of the dust, in the keen
    cool rush of the air,
  Under the flying white clouds, and broad blue lift
    of the sky;

And to halt at the chattering brook, in the tall green
    fern at the brink
  Where the harebell grows, and the gorse, and the
    fox-gloves purple and white;
Where the shy-eyed delicate deer troop down to the
    pools to drink,
  When the stars are mellow and large at the coming
    on of the night.

O! to feel the warmth of the rain, and the homely smell
    of the earth,
  Is a tune for the blood to jig to, a joy past power
    of words;
And the blessed green comely meadows seem all a-ripple
    with mirth
  At the lilt of the shifting feet, and the dear wild
    cry of the birds.

JOHN MASEFIELD

In Flanders

I'm homesick for my hills again –
   My hills again!
To see above the Severn plain
Unscabbarded against the sky
The blue high blade of Cotswold lie;
The giant clouds go royally
By jagged Malvern with a train
Of shadows. Where the land is low
Like a huge imprisoning O
I hear a heart that's sound and high,
I hear the heart within me cry:
'I'm homesick for my hills again –
   My hills again!
Cotswold or Malvern, sun or rain!
   My hills again!'

F.W. HARVEY

from *June*

O June, O June, that we desired so,
Wilt thou not make us happy on this day?
Across the river thy soft breezes blow
Sweet with the scent of beanfields far away,
Above our heads rustle the aspens grey,
Calm is the sky with harmless clouds beset,
No thought of storm the morning vexes yet.

See, we have left our hopes and fears behind
To give our very hearts up unto thee;
What better place than this then could we find
By this sweet stream that knows not of the sea,
That guesses not the city's misery,
This little stream whose hamlets scarce have names,
This far-off, lonely mother of the Thames?

WILLIAM MORRIS

Cotswolds

So much sky, and light, striking the stone
and green uplands. Crow and cloud-shadow
drift and wheel; sheep and farms in the folds.

Tumuli, spires, rutted tracks – relics
of older ways. Bones, fossils, quarries
breaching the skin. And the wind, always.

Nettles nod at stiles; orchids surprise
where cattle graze; and on darkening slopes
beeches stir and moan, splintering the sun. ·

A land for the solitary; pungent
in twilight; framed by mullion, lych-gate,
barn door; the silver river beyond.

DAVID ASHBEE

East Wind

Cool air moves there up on Cotswold edge,
By Crickley's bastion or the Shurdington wedge,
Grey grass rustles, the harebells dance and the east
Wind has no good influences on the cattle at feast.

Naked land-slides show, away down hill mist-shades cover
The land where South-West once moved high like a lover,
With colour and boy's glory and breath of renewal:
That also, that valley, for this dry air is a fuel.

But the great steeps keep one in right hoping still,
Mighty the upstanding curving of the golden-crowned hill
Crickley, where scabious and serious thistle nods,
And there is good hiding place for the old gods.

IVOR GURNEY

June Evening, Stroud Valley

Evening light slants over the valley
swallows balance and skim;
their forked tails flick
and the pale bellies gleam
like fish in the stream.

Trees lay down long shadows
on meadows shaven and pale;
against dark clouds
white dove wings shiver
like flowers in the river.

A shoulder of hill stands dark
above the clustering town;
the thin spire catches light
and its gold bird glitters
like a jewel in the waters.

SHEILA SIMMONS

The Villain

While joy gave clouds the light of stars,
    That beamed where'er they looked;
And calves and lambs had tottering knees,
    Excited, while they sucked;
While every bird enjoyed his song,
Without one thought of harm or wrong –
I turned my head and saw the wind,
    Not far from where I stood,
Dragging the corn by her golden hair,
    Into a dark and lonely wood.

W.H. DAVIES

Legacy

When twice a hundred years have gone
   Across my Cotswold eaves,
And still the woods of Sapperton
   Make summer of green leaves,
Come then and sing what song you will,
   You lovers of new time,
But sometimes on my Cotswold hill
   Renew my Cotswold rhyme.

Make me a temple on this ground
   Not built of mortal stone,
But sprung from unforgotten sound
   Of song my blood has known,
So shall my tale not be of dust
   Chilled in a common urn,
While proudly through your younger lust
   My testament shall burn.

JOHN DRINKWATER

Cotswold Ways

One comes across the strangest things in walks:
Fragments of Abbey tithe-barns fixed in modern
And Dutch-sort houses where the water baulks
Weired up, and brick kilns broken among fern,
Old troughs, great stone cisterns bishops might have blessed
Ceremonially, and worthy mounting-stones;
Black timber in red brick, queerly placed
Where Hill stone was looked for – and a manor's bones
Spied in the frame of some wisteria'd house
And mill-falls and sedge pools and Saxon faces;
Stream-sources happened upon in unlikely places,
And Roman-looking hills of small degree
And the surprise of dignity of poplars
At a road end, or the white Cotswold scars,
Or sheets spread white against the hazel tree.
Strange the large difference of up-Cotswold ways;
Birdlip climbs bold and treeless to a bend,
Portway to dim wood-lengths without end,
And Crickley goes to cliffs are the crown of days.

IVOR GURNEY

Briar Roses

High on Brockworth Common,
    Where the west winds blow,
Mass the sweet briar roses,
    Drifts of fragrant snow.
Creamy, dreamy roses,
    Fresh as morning's birth,
Bridal veils of sweetness
    Flung across the earth.

All among the roses
    Stray the browsing sheep,
In a sea of roses
    Lost and hidden deep.
Tangled, spangled roses,
    Rioting at will,
Heaped in warm white glory
    Over all the hill.

Starry through the twilight,
    When the sunset dies,
Gleam the wan-sweet roses,
    'Neath the fading skies.
Twining, shining roses,
    Filling all the air
With the rich dim incense
    Of their evening prayer.

EVA DOBELL

The High-Road

The little roads are quaint roads
    That wander where they will,
They wind their arms round all the farms
    And flirt with every hill;
But the high-road is my road
    And goes where I would go,
Its way it wends as man intends,
    For it was fashioned so,

The little roads are shy roads
    And care not to be seen,
'Twixt hedges hid they wind amid
    A labyrinth of green,
But the high-roads are bold roads
    And stare one in the face,
With banners white in all men's sight
    The land they proudly pace.

The little roads are faint roads
    And fear to walk alone,
They like the looks of friendly brooks
    And cots of county stone,
But the high-roads are proud roads
    And Lord it like the King,
They stride the dale the hills to scale,
    O'er wasting rivers they prevail,
Nor yield to anything.

To all the little roads I know
    Delightful haunts belong –
In hidden state lurks Stanway gate
    The Stanway woods among,
The river walk between the Colnes
    From Fosseway lies apart,
While Slaughter seems amid its streams
    To dwell in willow-pattern dreams
Dreamt by a childish heart.

But give me on an autumn day
    That Lordly road to trace
From Charlton Hill to Baunton Mill
    And Ciceter market place,
Or back, the way the Romans came
    Above a folded world
To Birdlip steep, where in a leap
    The road doth to that valley sweep
Where Severn lies unfurled.

The little roads are warm roads
    And fine to house within;
They grow great trees, escape the breeze
    And nurse the homely inn;
The high-roads are dry roads
    For many a thirsty mile,
But their wind and rain
    I will face again
As I have done many a while.

JOHN HAINES

In Painswick Churchyard

'Is this where people are buried?
I will not let them bury you'

He picnics among tombs
– pours imaginary tea,
a yew tree his kitchen

'You will live with me in my house'

Oh could I believe the living and dead inhabit one house
                              under the sky
and you my child run into your future for ever

FRANCES HOROVITZ

Dover's Hill

(to F.L. Griggs)

From this hill where the air's so clear
  We can see away and away,
And the villages, far as near,
  Shine in the lucid day.
On rough short grass we tread
  And thistles bend at our feet
And a lark sings overhead
  And the clouds are white and fleet.
The wind is strong in our faces,
  It drives us, we veer and yield,
And a broken thistle-top races
  Over the tossing field;
But below, as we look around,
  The deep long plains appear
Like a lost country drowned
  In a tranquil flood of air,
Whence now and again there rises
  To the listener on this shore
The muffled sound of the voices
  Of bells that ring once more.

EDWARD SHANKS

Adlestrop

Yes. I remember Adlestrop –
The name, because one afternoon
Of heat the express-train drew up there
Unwontedly. It was late June.

The steam hissed. Someone cleared his throat.
No one left and no one came
On the bare platform. What I saw
Was Adlestrop – only the name

And willows, willow-herb, and grass,
And meadowsweet, and haycocks dry,
No whit less still and lonely fair
Than the high cloudlets in the sky.

And for that minute a blackbird sang
Close by, and round him, mistier,
Farther and farther, all the birds
Of Oxfordshire and Gloucestershire.

EDWARD THOMAS

Milkmaid

The girl's far treble, muted to the heat,
calls like a fainting bird across the fields
to where her flock lies panting for her voice,
their black horns buried deep in marigolds.

They climbed awake, like drowsy butterflies,
and press their red flanks through the tall branched grass,
and as they go their wandering tongues embrace
the vacant summer mirrored in their eyes.

Led to the limestone shadows of a barn
they snuff their past embalmèd in the hay,
while her cool hand, cupped to the udder's fount,
distils the brimming harvest of their day.

Look what a cloudy cream the earth gives out,
fat juice of buttercups and meadow-rye;
the girl dreams milk within her body's field
and hears, far off, her muted children cry.

LAURIE LEE

Up There

On Cotswold edge there is a field and that
Grows thick with corn and speedwell and the mat
Of thistles, of the tall kind; Rome lived there,
Some hurt centurion got his grant or tenure,
Built farm with fowls and pigsties and wood-piles,
Waited for service custom between whiles.
The farmer ploughs up coins in the wet-earth-time,
He sees them on the topple of crests gleam,
Or run down furrow; and halts and does let them lie
Like a small black island in brown immensity,
Till his wonder is ceased, and his great hand picks up the penny.
Red pottery easy discovered, no searching needed . . .
One wonders what farms were like, no searching needed,
As now the single kite hovering still
By the coppice there, level with the flat of the hill.

IVOR GURNEY

from *Midsummer Morning Jog Log*

... Ah – holla there – silent
Sunflower!   Forget-me-not   – your smiles
   light up   the soul of the world
   my soul belongs to, now   I forget not you
and begin   to look – and perceive
the one unbounded   primeval garden – its seeds
and springs   like first light   – never lost
   since the very first dawn

... begin   to listen, and hear   again
   distantly   gathering trills
of the unending concert   of spiritual sensation
in which I apprehend   all our steps are envelopt

   ... like the petalfaced   grenades of pollen
– like nectaries   poised to exude   honeydew,
ambrosia ... of   *'that sweet golden clime'* –
that gleams   in Samuel Palmer's vaulted sheepscapes
   raining amber light from Cotswold stone
   through happy fields, here and now
– celestial in the sense of wordless   but grounded

   ... like these gaggles   of new lambs exploring
their enormous orchard   straining wobbly legs
for precedence   at the fleecy private bar
   – like these blotchy bevies   of bullocks
that snort   at tough tussocks and sheepdogs
and joggers and wasps ...

MICHAEL HOROVITZ

51

Cotswold Roads

Those broad hill roads that lead away
   Dusty and white, with margins wide
Of grass and myriad upland flowers –
   Jewelled bands on either side.

Great beds of trefoil golden bright,
   And slender harebells, clear and frail,
Scabious, and milk-wort pearly pure
   Rock-roses, primrose-pale.

The wild geraniums' fragrant tide
   Massed clouds of such celestial hue,
The very sky seems fallen there
   In drifts of azure blue.

And still the broad white road leads on
   To some grey village, nestled deep
In the hill's dimple, where the elms
   Seem sentries dropped asleep.

A Cotswold village that has dozed
   For centuries thus grey and old,
Under the slope that breaks the wind
   That sweeps across the wold.

The wind that sweeps across the wold,
   Where dried bents whiten to the sky,
And like the voice of silence flits
   The lapwing's wheeling cry.

And over hill and barren wold,
   Where sun and fleet cloud shadows play,
The white roads that the Romans trod
   Still hold their ancient way.

EVA DOBELL

Gloucestershire From The Train

The golden fields wheel round –
  Their spokes, green hedges;
And at the galloping sound
  Of the train, from watery sedges
    Arise familiar birds.

Pools brown, and blue, and green,
  Criss-crossed with shadows,
Flash by, and in between
  Gloucestershire meadows
    Lie speckled red with herds.

A little flying farm,
  With humped grey back
Against the rays that warm
  To gold a last-year stack,
    Like a friendly cat appears;

And so through gloom and gleam
  Continues dwindling,
While in my heart a dream
  Of home awakes to kindling
    Fire, and falling tears.

                    F.W. HARVEY

Quiet Talk

Tree-talk is breathing quietly today
Of coming autumn and the staleness over –
Pause of high summer when the year's at stay,
And the wind's sick that now moves like a lover.

On valley ridges where our beeches cluster
Or changing ashes guarding slopes of plough,
He goes now sure of heart, now with a fluster
Of teasing purpose. Night shall find him grow

To dark strength and a cruel spoiling will.
First he will baffle streams and dull their bright,
Cower and threaten both about the hill –
Before their death trees have their full delight.

IVOR GURNEY

AUTUMN

Swift Beauty

Wind that is in orchards
    Playing with apple-trees
Soon will be leagues away
    In the old rookeries.

Vaguely it arises,
    Swiftly it hurries hence: –
Like sudden beauty
    Blown over sense:

Like all unheeded
    Beautiful things that pass
Under the leaves of life,
    Just touching the grass.

            F.W. HARVEY

from *Dedicatory Ode*

The quiet evening kept her tryst:
Beneath an open sky we rode,
And passed into a wandering mist
Along the perfect Evenlode.

The tender Evenlode that makes
Her meadows hush to hear the sound
Of waters mingling in the brakes,
And binds my heart to English ground.

A lovely river, all alone,
She lingers in the hills and holds
A hundred little towns of stone,
Forgotten in the western wolds.

            HILAIRE BELLOC

Cotswold Lad

The farm remains he laboured on
   And cherished like a lover;
The land remains but he is gone;
   The sunlit days are over.

He was most loyal and a friend
   With gentle ways of giving,
He took the blows that fate can send
   As well as any living.

He loved the hills that were his home,
   He loved sunrise and setting;
He loved to see the green corn come,
   He loved the harvest getting.

Where fields are girt with Cotswold stone,
   Where Cotswold kind go reaping,
Among the folk he called his own
   The Cotswold lad is sleeping.

FRANK MANSELL

Apples

Behold the apples' rounded worlds:
juice-green of July rain,
the black polestar of flowers, the rind
mapped with its crimson stain.

The russet, crab and cottage red
burn to the sun's hot brass,
then drop like sweat from every branch
and bubble in the grass.

They lie as wanton as they fall,
and where they fall and break,
the stallion clamps his crunching jaws,
the starling stabs his beak.

In each plump gourd the cidery bite
of boys' teeth tears the skin;
the waltzing wasp consumes his share,
the bent worm enters in.

I, with as easy hunger, take
entire my season's dole;
welcome the ripe, the sweet, the sour,
the hollow and the whole.

LAURIE LEE

from *The Story of the Glittering Plain*

Fair is the world, now autumn's wearing
And the sluggard sun lies long abed;
Sweet are the days, now winter's nearing,
And all the winds feign that the wind is dead.

Dumb is the hedge where the crabs hang yellow,
Bright as the blossoms of the spring;
Dumb is the close where the pears grow mellow,
And none but the dauntless redbreasts sing.

Fair was the spring, but amidst his greening
Grey were the days of the hidden sun;
Fair was the summer, but overweaning,
So soon his o'er-sweet days were done.

Come then, love, for peace is upon us,
Far off is failing, and far is fear,
Here where the rest in the end hath won us,
In the garnering tide of the happy year.

Come from the grey old house by the water,
Where, far from the lips of the hungry sea,
Green groweth the grass o'er the field of the slaughter,
And all is a tale for thee and me.

WILLIAM MORRIS

from *Songs of the Three Rivers*

(from *The Island*)

Yet rare and fugitive, hour by hour,
Fade on the moving mirror's face
The imaged beauty of Worcester tower
And Tewkesbury tower, and the stony lace
Of Gloucester's fretted parapet;
And the mournful stone of Berkeley's keep
Saddens her surface – but not yet
Shall dreaming Severn awake from sleep,
Not till the green vale opens wide
And the wrath of the bore rolls in from sea
And the stinging salt of the sudden tide
Mindeth her of her destiny.

FRANCIS BRETT YOUNG

September

She walketh like a ghost,
  Lovely and gray
And faint, faint, faint . . .
  Ere Autumn's host
Of colours gay
  Breaks on the year, September
Comes sighing her soft plaint,
  'Remember!'

Remember what? All fair
  Warm loves now wan:
All fleet, fleet, fleet
  Flowers in the hair
Of Summers gone!
  Though fruit break rosy, of these
Are her most sweet
  Sad memories.

Most faint and tender
  Music awaketh,
Sighing, sighing, sighing,
  A voice to lend her.
Surely it breaketh
  Even Death's heart, as he goes
To gather in Summer's long-dying
  Last rose.

So drifting like a ghost,
  Lovely with dream
And faint, faint, faint,
  Sighing 'remember', almost
September did seem
  My gray soul's image, as she
Whispered over that plaint
  So musically!

F. W. HARVEY

This Ancient Wall

This ancient wall of Cotswold stone
Has listened low to every storm,
Whose murmurs through her crevices
Sang softly to the mighty trees
She sheltered once in infant form.
From youth she saw these monarchs grow
To giants, whose deep serenade
Cast about her honoured bones
Their wealth of cooling shade.
Beside these trees and moss-grown stones
A wearied traveller loved to rest
And was the wall's appointed guest.
Last night the tempest swept the wold
And wracked the trees whose music smote
A sound so old, yet strangely new,
Out of each muscle, bone and thew
Into the wall's deep throat.
She felt their roots beneath her feet
Quiver and creak like beasts afraid,
Who cower under storms of sleet
When thunder loosens lightning's blade.
Five trunks of wood on scattered stone,
Five breaches in a ruined wall,
Bear witness of the muffled groan
She uttered at these loved one's fall.

BRIAN WATERS

Have Wandered

When I think of cool woods in the sunlight,
Dark avenues trembling with song,
And sheep running wild in the bracken,
I know that I cannot look backwards
Nor tread any road of my childhood,
How far I have wandered.

And when I consider bright Severn
That wound through the orchards and farms,
And barley out-topping the hedges,
I know that the old days are done with,
The corn and the ripe fruit long gathered,
How far I have wandered.

When I walk through the fog in this north land
And remember the clear hills of home
That crouched round the white tower of Gloucester,
I know I am locked in a prison
And lost in my own fog for ever,
How far I have wandered.

How far have I wandered?
From the source to the sea of my making,
From the ebb and the flow of my waking,
From the pain and the joy of my growing,
From the heart and the head of my knowing;
Thus far have I wandered.

LEONARD CLARK

Field of Autumn

Slow moves the acid breath of noon
over the copper-coated hill,
slow from the wild crab's bearded breast
the palsied apples fall.

Like coloured smoke the day hangs fire,
taking the village without sound;
the vulture-headed sun lies low
chained to the violet ground.

The horse upon the rocky height
rolls all the valley in his eye,
but dares not raise his foot or move
his shoulder from the fly.

The sheep, snail-backed against the wall,
lifts her blind face but does not know
the cry her blackened tongue gives forth
is the first bleat of snow.

Each bird and stone, each roof and well,
feels the gold foot of autumn pass;
each spider binds with glittering snare
the splintered bones of grass.

Slow moves the hour that sucks our life,
slow drops the late wasp from the pear,
the rose tree's thread of scent draws thin –
and snaps upon the air.

LAURIE LEE

Cotswold Tiles

The finest roofs in all the land are made from Cotswold stone,
And the mason gives each tile a name like children of his own.
By length and breadth the tally runs, by width and depth and size,
And the mason knows them all by name, for he is very wise.

Long Day, Short Day, Moreday and Muffity,
Lye-byes and Bottomers, each a name receives:
Wivett, Beck, and Cussomes, Cutting, Third and Bachelor,
Smallest under roof-ridge, largest over eaves.

Each tile in its own special place is hung with loving care,
And they weather down the ages in the mellow Cotswold air:
Twenty-six in all there are – the family's not small,
I can but tell you one or two, I can't remember all.

Long Day, Short Day, Moreday and Muffity,
Lye-byes and Bottomers, each a name receives:
Wivett, Beck and Cussomes, Cutting, Third and Bachelor,
Smallest under roof-ridge, largest over eaves.

EDWARD BERRYMAN

Roel Gate

I love to walk the secret ways of prehistoric man,
Where scratched across the Cotswold Hills the ancient trackways ran.
The cattle ways, the salt ways, the lonely pilgrim's ride
To the hinterland of England from silver Severnside.

I wonder if these ancient folk had time to stand and stare,
Saw beauty in the rolling hills and loved the upland air;
Gazed eastward over English plains to watch the morning rise,
Or lingered long on Birdlip Hill to gaze at sunset skies.

Perhaps they made these upland ways with nothing more in mind
Than to escape the hazards of the plains they left behind.
But glad I am they ran them on skylines lifted high
Where we may walk on quiet hills beneath a Cotswold sky.

And best of all, the ancient way that climbs by Salter's Hill
To ride a world of sky and wind where time is standing still.
Here by the lonely Roel Gate where fields fade into sky,
Here on the roof of Cotswold I touch eternity.

ARTHUR DALBY

The Cotswold Farmers

Sometimes the ghosts forgotten go
 Along the hill-top way,
And with long scythes of silver mow
 Meadows of moonlit hay,
Until the cocks of Cotswold crow
 The coming of the day.

There's Tony Turkletob who died
 When he could drink no more,
And Uncle Heritage, the pride
 Of eighteen-twenty-four,
And Ebenezer Barleytide,
 And others half a score.

They fold in phantom pens, and plough
 Furrows without a share,
And one will milk a faery cow,
 And one will stare and stare,
And whistle ghostly tunes that now
 Are not sung anywhere.

The moon goes down on Oakridge lea,
 The other world's astir,
The Cotswold farmers silently
 Go back to sepulchre,
The sleeping watchdogs wake, and see
 No ghostly harvester.

JOHN DRINKWATER

Old Martinmas Eve

The moon, one tree, one star.
Still meadows far,
Enwreathed and scarfed by phantom lines of white.
November's night
Of all her nights, I thought, and turned to see
Again that moon and star-supporting tree.
If some most quiet tune had spoken then;
Some silver thread of sound; a core within
That sea-deep silentness, I had not known
Ever such joy in peace, but sound was none –
Nor should be till birds roused to find the dawn.

IVOR GURNEY

November Eves

November Evenings! Damp and still
They used to cloak Leckhampton hill,
And lie down close on the grey plain,
And dim the dripping window-pane,
And send queer winds like Harlequins
That seized our elms for violins
And struck a note so sharp and low
Even a child could feel the woe.

Now fire chased shadow round the room;
Tables and chairs grew vast in gloom:
We crept about like mice, while Nurse
Sat mending, solemn as a hearse,
And even our unlearned eyes
Half closed with choking memories.

Is it the mist or the dead leaves,
Or the dead men – November eves?

JAMES ELROY FLECKER

Walking in Autumn

(for Diana Lodge)

We have overshot the wood.
The track has led us beyond trees
to the tarmac edge. Too late now
at dusk to return a different way,
hazarding barbed wire or an unknown bull.
We turn back onto the darkening path.
Pale under-leaves of whitebeam, alder
gleam at our feet like stranded fish
or Hansel's stones.
A wren, unseen, churrs alarm:
each tree drains to blackness.
Halfway now, we know
by the leaning crab-apple,
feet crunching into mud
the hard slippery yellow moons.
We hurry without reason
stumbling over roots and stones.
A night creature lurches, cries out,
crashes through brambles.
Skin shrinks inside our clothes;
almost we run
falling through darkness to the wood's end,
the gate into the sloping field.
Home is lights and woodsmoke, voices –
and, our breath caught, not trembling now,
a strange reluctance to enter within doors.

FRANCES HOROVITZ

A Ghost of Summer

Where O where will wildness go
Now the sunshine turns to snow

The cold winds blow my spirits low
 The high winds call my spirit back

To flow and run – and ebb, for lack
Of clear direction. Alone I walk

Through empty streets, I talk
To no one – none else abroad

 My pumping heart awaits the hoard
Must needs reward me at the next hilltop

But mounted to the crest I stop
Aghast – no promised land in harvest there

Instead a maze of prostrate trees, picked bare
– Derelict dwellings – Where went the crop?

 A labyrinth of ruined fields that tear
My hope out

 – Unidentified am I
A last seed blown nowhere by the wintry sky

MICHAEL HOROVITZ

Autumn Swan Song

The pale cascades of Autumn sunlight
Ripple through the interlacing fingers of a
    chestnut tree
Reflecting muted hues of red and gold.
Patterns criss-cross, showing stark against the
    back-drop of a smoky sky.
A dying leaf floats silently towards the
    waiting earth,
The stealthy, creeping mists enshroud the
    countryside
Erasing scenery, like soft grey curtains
    drawn across a lighted window.
And Autumn – having nearly played her part,
Picks up her ragged skirts for one more bow
While winter waits and watches in the wings.

JOYCE LATHAM

Elemental

A last flame,
sole leaf
flagging at the tree tip,
is dragged through the current
down into the water
of the air, and in this final
metamorphosis, spiralling
swims to earth.

CHARLES TOMLINSON

WINTER

Last Leaf

What binds the last sere leaf to the winter tree
When all the rest are loosed reluctantly?
Bludgeoned by hail,
Torn in the mindless gale,
Ground in degrading mud,
Flown to the flood,
Curled in the morning frost,
The whispering legion of the lately lost,
They end their being
Humiliated 'ghosts from an enchanter fleeing'.

What ties tormented twig and the lone leaf together?
Perhaps shared days of 'blue unclouded weather'.

JIM TURNER

On Buying OS Sheet 163

I own all this. Not loutish acres
That tax the spirit, but the hawking
Eye's freehold, paper country.

Thirtytwo inches of aqueduct,
Windmill (disused), club house, embankment,
Public conveniences

In rural areas. This is my
Landlocked landscape that lives in cipher,
And is truer than walking.

Red and imperial, the Romans
Stride eastward. Mysterious, yellow,
The Salt Way halts and is gone.

Here, bigger than the hamlets they are,
Wild wayside syllables stand blooming:
Filkins, Lechlade, Broughton Poggs.

Here only I discard the umber
Reticulations of sad cities,
The pull and drag of mud.

U.A. FANTHORPE

from *Cider-House*

Only a few remember the cider days,
the shuffle of clogged feet on the littered floor,
fruit piled high in the round baskets,
trundled in from the warm harvesting,
the nodding horses waiting patiently by the orchard gate,
waggons bumping along the ruts to the cool house.

And then all day the golden liquid
trickling, bubble and drop, through the creaking wood,
the engine still humming the same, soft song,
pipes, hogsheads, and puncheons filled to the bung,
the raw juice heady, overflowing,
mashed straw and pulp thrown to the pigs.

They are gone now, cider-house and orchards,
the billowing tides of blossoms riding the slopes,
with early bees raiding, and Severn, a silver eel,
twisting to the sea on the far-away skyline.

The magical names remain,
those old apples of cidered Gloucestershire,
Skyrmes Kernel, Dymock Red, and Forest Styre,
Black Foxwhelps and Redstreak;
such honeyed sounds,
pure English poetry in my country ears.
I say each one to myself now, lovely on my tongue,
as ripe and rounded as cider itself,
drunk with long memories from a china mug,
the fire glowing on a winter evening.

LEONARD CLARK

Old Man's Beard

What we failed to see
was twines of the wild clematis
climbing all summer
through each burdened tree:

not till the leaves were gone
did we begin to take
the measure of what strength
had fed from the limestone

that roof of feathered seed
bearding the woods now
in its snowy foliage
yet before fall of snow

and what silent cordage bound
the galaxy together where
December light reflected
from star on hairy star

innumerably united
in a cascade, a cloud, a wing
to hang their canopy above
the roots they were strangling.

CHARLES TOMLINSON

Springtime in December

The wind blows chill on Dunkite Hill
   But deep below in Dillay,
And all along the valley floor
   From Famish Springs to Elcombe,
The Slad Brook pipes an April tune
   To bid the stranger welcome.

December on the Bisley Road,
   But April in my valley.
Below the darkling Piedmont height
   The air is warm in welcome
As evening sunshine turns the hill
   To kiss the roofs of Elcombe.

When earth grows cold, and I'm too old
   To seek the paths from Dillay,
Then as I dream beside the fire
   My glad heart will remember
That there beside the quiet Slad
   Is springtime in December.

ARTHUR DALBY

Singing in the Streets

I had almost forgotten the singing in the streets,
Snow piled up by the houses, drifting
Underneath the door into the warm room,
Firelight, lamplight, the little lame cat
Dreaming in soft sleep on the hearth, mother dozing,
Waiting for Christmas to come, the boys and me
Trudging over blanket fields waving lanterns to the sky.
I had almost forgotten the smell, the feel of it all,
The coming back home, with girls laughing like stars,
Their cheeks, holly berries, me kissing one,
Silent-tongued, soberly, by the long church wall;
Then back to the kitchen table, supper on the white cloth,
Cheese, bread, the home made wine,
Symbols of the night's joy, a holy feast.
And I wonder now, years gone, mother gone,
The boys and girls scattered, drifted away with the snowflakes,
Lamplight done, firelight over,
If the sounds of our singing in the streets are still there,
Those old tunes, still praising;
And now, a lifetime of Decembers away from it all,
A branch of remembering holly stabs my cheeks,
And I think it may be so;
Yes, I believe it may be so.

LEONARD CLARK

Christmas Landscape

Tonight the wind gnaws
with teeth of glass,
the jackdaw shivers
in caged branches of iron,
the stars have talons.

There is hunger in the mouth
of vole and badger,
silver agonies of breath
in the nostril of the fox,
ice on the rabbit's paw.

Tonight has no moon,
no food for the pilgrim;
the fruit tree is bare,
the rose bush a thorn
and the ground bitter with stones.

But the mole sleeps, and the hedgehog
lies curled in a womb of leaves,
the bean and the wheat-seed
hug their germs in the earth
and the stream moves under the ice.

Tonight there is no moon,
but a new star opens
like a silver trumpet over the dead.
Tonight in a nest of ruins
the blessèd babe is laid.

And the fir tree warms to a bloom of candles,
the child lights his lantern,
stares at his tinselled toy;
our hearts and hearths
smoulder with live ashes.

In the blood of our grief
the cold earth is suckled,
in our agony the womb
convulses its seed,
in the last cry of anguish
the child's first breath is born.

LAURIE LEE

Resolution at the New Year

Children drag home through dusk,
week-old snow brown in hedgerows,
a full moon slices the wood.

Somewhere spring is gathering its green,
star gives place to climbing star
(they too have grown older).

I shall not be careless this year:
I shall not forget to see the wild garlic blossom
– as I did last May, and the May before.

FRANCES HOROVITZ

News from Gloucestershire

This snow, thaw, frost, thaw and rain
Has bitten great gaps in the old limestone
Walls that summer visitors delighted in:
Dark grey, with rusty orange and sky-grey lichen
And mosses green as cress; they caught the sun
Pink in the morning and, white under the moon,
Shadowed the fox. They have fallen down.

Nor will be, nor should be, built again,
Fences being cheaper; they are done
That were my passion. Foxes' navigation, weasels' run,
Skilful catchers of every light, they open
Like graves, a jumble of yellow bone
That tractors tidy away. Visitors from the town
May vaguely remark an absence, travel on.

The thud, thud, is fence-posts going in.

P.J. KAVANAGH

from *The Everlasting Mercy*

Near Bullen Bank, on Gloucester Road,
Thy everlasting mercy showed
The ploughman patient on the hill
For ever there, for ever still,
Ploughing the hill with steady yoke
Of pine-trees lightning-struck and broke.
I've marked the May Hill ploughman stay
There on his hill, day after day
Driving his team against the sky,
While men and women live and die.
And now and then he seems to stoop
To clear the coulter with the scoop,
Or touch an ox to haw or gee
While Severn stream goes out to sea.
The sea with all her ships and sails,
And that great smoky port in Wales,
And Gloucester tower bright i' the sun,
All know that patient wandering one.

JOHN MASEFIELD

Winter

An open gate, a field new ploughed,
  The wind north-east upon the hill;
A naked copse, an old man bowed,
  Who walks the road with time to kill;

Who climbs the hill as dusk comes down
  And thinks of days he used to know,
Whose mind is like a lighted town
  Under the lamps of long ago.

FRANK MANSELL

The Brassrubbing

The Unknown Sheepman at Northleach
and his Unknown Wife have been sleeping in
the same stone bed for more than 400
years Both are fully clothed He is always
the perfect gentleman Sheep explain
his success His unknown wife
lies perfectly still with hands crossed
in prayer But he cannot touch her
Lord I have covered her body with paper
rubbing until nipples again shine through
in the exhausted cold at Northleach
we go about our business Whilst the
sheepman dreams of the brass he has made
and the fleecing that remains to be done

LES ARNOLD

Nailsworth Hill

The Moon, that peeped as she came up,
   Is clear on top, with all her light;
She rests her chin on Nailsworth Hill,
   And, where she looks, the World is white.

White with her light – or is it Frost,
   Or is it Snow her eyes have seen;
Or is it Cherry blossom there,
   Where no such trees have ever been?

W.H. DAVIES

In The Balance

The cold came. It has photographed the scene
With so exact a care, that you can look
From field-white and from wood-black to the air
Now that the snow has ceased, and catch no shade
Except these three – the third is the sky's grey:
Will it thicken or thaw, this rawness menacing?
The sky stirs: the sky refuses to say:
But it lets new colour in: its thinning smoke
Opens towards a region beyond snow,
Rifts to a blueness rather than a blue:
Brought to a sway, the whole day hesitates
Through the sky of afternoon, and you beneath,
As if questions of weather were of life and death.

CHARLES TOMLINSON

The High Hills

The high hills have a bitterness
Now they are not known
And memory is poor enough consolation
For the soul hopeless gone.
Up in the air there beech tangles wildly in the wind –
That I can imagine
But the speed, the swiftness, walking into clarity,
Like last year's bryony are gone.

IVOR GURNEY

Triolet

Winter has hardened all the ground,
  But flowers are on the window-pane;
No others are there to be found: –
Winter has hardened all the ground.
But here, while Earth is bare and bound,
  Bloom ghosts of those his frost has slain.
Winter has hardened all the ground,
  But flowers are on the window-pane.

F.W. HARVEY

Cotswold Choice

By Honeycombe and Henley
By Sapperton and Syde
By Climperwell enchanted
Where magic waters bide

By Wishanger and Winston
By Camp and Caudle Green
By Battlescombe and Bisley
In quest of love I've been

By Miserden and Morcombe
By Stancombe and by Slad
By Eastcombe and by Elcombe
Gay have I gone and sad

By Througham Fields and Tunley
By Detcombe and the Dell
By Lypiatt and Longridge
Hang tales too long to tell

Oh, Bunnage, Bidfield, Birdlip,
Buckholt and Cranham Knoll
From Paradise to Painswick
At times I've loved them all

At times I've loved them all, lad,
But if by chance I die
Then set me down in Sheepscombe
In Sheepscombe I would lie.

FRANK MANSELL

Boy in Ice

O river, green and still,
By frost and memory stayed,
Your dumb and stiffened glass divides
A shadow and a shade.

In air, the shadow's face
My winter gaze lets fall
To see beneath the stream's bright bars
That other shade in thrall.

A boy, time-fixed in ice,
His cheeks with summer dyed,
His mouth, a rose-devouring rose,
His bird-throat petrified.

O fabulous and lost,
More distant to me now
Than rock-drawn mammoth, painted stag
Or tigers in the snow.

You stare into my face
Dead as ten thousand years,
Your sparrow tongue sealed in my mouth
Your world about my ears.

And till our shadows meet,
Till time burns through the ice,
Thus frozen shall we ever stay
Locked in this paradise.

LAURIE LEE

This Night The Stars

This night the stars like jewels shine
   High over Birdlip Hill,
And Severn's but a silvery line
   Smooth flowing at her will,
While all the lamps of Gloucester Town
Are twinkling and the moon-beams down
   Upon these fields of mine.

How can this ever pass away,
   This home of hills and trees?
I rather think on Judgement Day,
   When all are on their knees,
They'll find who through the clouds shall rise
That Gloucestershire is Paradise,
   And Heaven's fields are these.

LEONARD CLARK

INDEX OF FIRST LINES

INDEX OF POETS

Information on Albums and Engravings

Albums

The following poems from this anthology have been set to music and recorded on these albums by Johnny Coppin:

On *Forest and Vale and High Blue Hill*:
'A Song of Gloucestershire', 'In Flanders', and 'Piper's Wood' by F.W. Harvey; 'Cotswold Love', 'Legacy', and 'The Cotswold Farmers' by John Drinkwater; 'Have Wandered', and 'This Night The Stars' by Leonard Clark; 'The Fisherman of Newnham' by Ivor Gurney; 'Field of Autumn' by Laurie Lee; 'Briar Roses' by Eva Dobell; 'The High-Road' by John Haines; 'Cotswold Lad' by Frank Mansell.

On *English Morning*:
'East Wind', and 'The High Hills' by Ivor Gurney; 'The Everlasting Mercy' by John Masefield; 'Dover's Hill' by Edward Shanks; 'The Hill' by Leonard Clark; 'Nailsworth Hill' by W.H. Davies; 'Cotswold Tiles' by Edward Berryman; 'Winter' by Frank Mansell.

On *Edge of Day* with Laurie Lee:
'The Edge of Day', and 'Apples'. The following are among those poems read by Laurie Lee: 'April Rise', 'Milkmaid', 'Field of Autumn', 'Christmas Landscape', and 'Boy in Ice'.

On *Glorious Glosters* with the Band of the Glos. Regiment:
'A Song of Gloucestershire' by F.W. Harvey; 'This Night The Stars' by Leonard Clark; 'The Roads Go Down' by Frank Mansell (also on *Roll on Dreamer* album)

On *Songs on Lonely Roads - The Story of Ivor Gurney*:
'The Fisherman of Newnham', and 'The High Hills' by Ivor Gurney; 'In Flanders' by F.W. Harvey.

Johnny Coppin Discography

with Decameron: *Say Hello To The Band* 1973. Vertigo 6360 097
Mammoth Special 1974. Mooncrest Crest 19
Third Light 1975. Transatlantic TRA 304
Tomorrow's Pantomime 1976. Transatlantic
TRA 325

Solo *Roll on Dreamer* 1978. Avada AVA 102
No Going Back 1979. Rola R 002
Get Lucky 1982. Starward SWL 2003
Forest and Vale and High Blue Hill 1983.
Red Sky. R 015/RSKC 015/RSKCD 015
Line of Blue 1985. Red Sky. RSK 106/RSKC
106
English Morning 1987. Red Sky. RSK 107/
RSKC 107
Edge of Day – with Laurie Lee 1989. Red Sky.
RSK 108/RSKC 108/RSKCD 108
The Glorious Glosters – with the Band of Glos.
Regiment 1990. Red Sky. RSK 109/RSKC
109
*Songs on Lonely Roads – The Story of Ivor
Gurney* (with David Goodland) 1990. Red
Sky. RSKC 110
West Country Christmas 1990. Red Sky. RSKC
111/RSKCD 111

All Johnny Coppin albums on Red Sky Records are available at good record shops (via CM Distribution) and by mail order direct from Red Sky Records. For a catalogue and price list please write to: Red Sky Records, P.O. Box 7, Stonehouse, Glos. GL10 3PQ, UK.

If you would like to be on the mailing list for news of future concerts, album releases, books etc., then please send your name and address to Red Sky Records.

Wood Engravings

Ray Hedger has incorporated a 'visual quote' in one of his engravings, the first person who can identify this (and give the name of the engraver, the book, and location of the original from which the quote comes) in writing to the publisher, will receive a free signed Artist's Proof of the engraving.

Prints from the original engraved wood blocks are available signed and numbered by the artist in a limited edition of 250. These can be obtained by sending an order with your name and address, together with a cheque to the publishers, The Windrush Press, Windrush House, 12 Main Street, Adlestrop, Moreton-in-Marsh, Glos. GL56 0YN. Tel: 0608 658075. Fax: 0608 658860. Please make cheques payable to Ray Hedger.

April Rise, Sonnet, Cotswold Ways, On Buying OS Sheet 163, This Night the Stars, £20.00 each (8″ × 5″ approx.).

Sezincote, Cotswold Lad, In March, Cotswolds, Winter, £15.00 each (4″ × 5″ approx.).

Title pages and vignettes £8.00 each (3″ × 3″ approx.).

Full set £180.00 (saving £59.00)